Discovering My World

Comets and Asteroids

by Melvin and Gilda Berger

SCHOLASTIC INC.

New York   Toronto   London   Auckland
Sydney   Mexico City   New Delhi   Hong Kong

ISBN 978-0-545-35166-9

12 11 10 9 8 7 6 5 4 3   13 14 15 16/0

Printed in the U.S.A.   40
First printing, November 2011

Photo Credits: Photo Research: Alan Gottlieb

Cover: © Triff/Shutterstock; Back cover: © Media Bakery; Title page: © Jerry Schad/Photo
Researchers, Inc.; Page 3: © Walter Dawn/Photo Researchers, Inc.; Page 4: © Richard Bizley/Photo
Researchers, Inc.; Page 5: © David Hardy/Photo Researchers, Inc.; Page 6: © Dale Darby/Photo Researchers,
Inc.; Page 7: © Karl Dolenc/iStockphoto; Page 8: European Southern Observatory; Page 9: Pekka
Parviainen/Photo Researchers, Inc.; Page 10: The Bridgeman Art Library; Page 11: JPL/NASA; Page
12: © Stocktrek Images/Getty Images; Page 13: © Lynette Cook/Photo Researchers, Inc.; Page
14: © Mehau Kulyk/Science Photo Library; Page 15: © Detlev van Ravenswaay/Science Photo
Library; Page 16: © Detlev van Ravenswaay/Photo Researchers, Inc.

Comets are large balls of ice and dust.

Comets travel around the sun like planets.

Can you trace this comet's path with your finger?

But they have much longer paths.

Sometimes a comet comes close to the sun.

What colors do you see in this comet's tail?

The heat of the sun melts the ice.

The ice forms a very long tail
of gas and dust.

Do you see all the stars?

The tail may stretch millions of miles.

People first saw Halley's comet
in the year 1066.

Does Halley's comet have a thick tail?

The same comet comes around
every 76 years.

Are all asteroids the same shape?

Asteroids are rocks that travel around the sun.

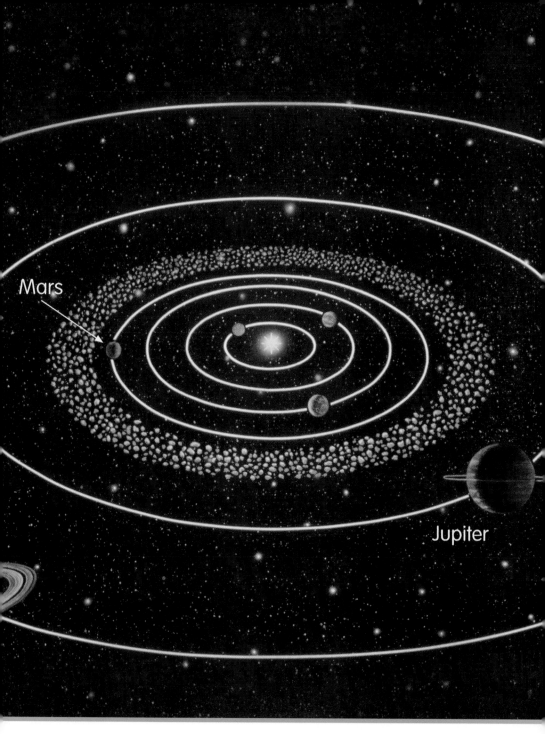

Mars

Jupiter

Most asteroids are found between Mars and Jupiter.

Small asteroids are the size of trucks.

Big ones are hundreds of miles across.

sk Yourself

1. What are comets?
2. Are comet tails long?
3. What is an asteroid?
4. Where are most asteroids found?
5. Are small asteroids the same size
   as trucks?

You can find the answers in this book.